WE HOLD
THE ROCK

THE INDIAN OCCUPATION OF ALCATRAZ, 1969 TO 1971

by Troy R. Johnson
Quotes by Veterans of the Occupation

GOLDEN GATE NATIONAL PARKS CONSERVANCY
SAN FRANCISCO, CALIFORNIA

ALCATRAZ RAIN

Throughout the cold and winter nights
We tended to our fires,
We drew our blankets close around
And watched the waves crash higher.

Though the cold waves beat on Alcatraz
Indian hearts are stout,
For white men think we'll go away—
But we'll live this winter out!

For the North Wind is our Brother;
We share his bitter shock;
Aii—we are the warriors of Alcatraz,
And we hold the Rock!

LONEWOLF, BLACKFOOT

THIS BOOK IS DEDICATED TO THE INDIANS OF ALCATRAZ,
AND TO THE GENERATIONS BEFORE AND THOSE THAT FOLLOW.

Alcatraz Island is now part of Golden Gate National Recreation Area. The story of the Indian occupation is an important part of its past, and one that the National Park Service wanted to make available to those visiting the island.

In response, in the fall and winter of 1996-1997, a multi-disciplinary team led by Jon Plutte of the Golden Gate National Parks Conservancy began interviewing on videotape a number of veterans of the 1969 occupation. From those tapes came the multimedia exhibit "We Hold the Rock," which opened on Alcatraz in the summer of 1997, and this publication. Included in this book are extracts from the interviews; any editorial changes to the individual's words are indicated with ellipses or brackets.

The goals of both the multimedia exhibit and the publication are to shed light on this landmark event in the American Indian struggle for human rights and to give visitors to Alcatraz a wider understanding of the island's role in American history. Members of the Indian community (both in the Bay Area and across the country), National Park Service interpreters and historians, and others committed to telling the story contributed to this project. Without their assistance, neither the exhibit nor the book would exist, and we thank all of them for their generosity of spirit and time.

Front cover: From left, Harold Patty, Paiute; Oohosis, Cree from Canada; and Peggy and friend at Pier 40 after the removal, June 11, 1971.
p. iii: Participants in the 1978 "Long Walk for Survival" to Washington, D.C., start their protest march with a traditional ceremony on Alcatraz.
Back cover: Alcatraz Island, June 1970

Second printing, 2007

Library of Congress Catalog Card Number 96-78731

ISBN-13: 978-188386928-1
ISBN-10: 188386928-5

The poem "Alcatraz Rain" by Lonewolf is used with permission of the author.

All quotes are drawn from contemporary 1996 and 1997 interviews; exceptions are dated.

Editors: Sandra Scott, Susan Tasaki
Consulting editors: Millie Ketcheshawno, Joseph Myers, Dennis Jennings
Printed in the United States
Design and Production: Reuter Design, www.reuterdesign.com

CONTENTS

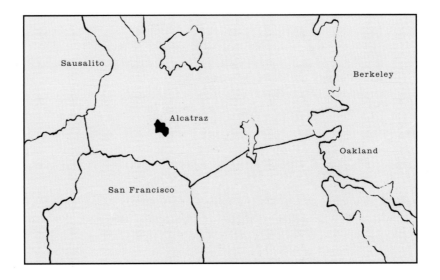

THIS IS THE BEGINNING OF OUR FIGHT FOR JUSTICE AND SELF-DETERMI-NATION.

RICHARD OAKES, MOHAWK (NOVEMBER 24, 1969)

Preface

"Who gets to tell the stories is a major issue of our time," says Elizabeth Cook-Lynn, member of the Crow Creek Sioux Tribe, scholar, and writer in her powerful book, *Why I Can't Read Wallace Stegner, and Other Essays.*

On the pages following, Indian American voices and white American voices tell their stories. It could be said that, although they walk the same path, they look in different directions, reflecting the truths that each person knew, felt, and lived.

It is impossible in a book this size and of this type to thoroughly cover the troubled history of Indian/Anglo American relations. We do, however, encourage you to seek out this history on your own. To use this work as a starting point. To hear the voices and feel the stories.

THE EDITORS

IMMEDIATELY FOLLOWING THE INDIAN WAR ERA, THERE BEGAN A SERIES OF GOVERN-MENT POLICIES THAT WERE DESIGNED TO MAKE SURE THAT WE DIDN'T EXIST ANYMORE AS TRIBAL PEOPLE. THAT WE NO LONGER HAD OUR LAN-GUAGE, OUR CULTURAL IDENTITY, OUR RELIGION, AND MOST IMPORTANTLY, OUR LAND AND NATURAL RESOURCES.

WILMA MANKILLER, CHEROKEE

INTRODUCTION

FOR THOUSANDS OF NATIVE PEOPLE, Alcatraz Island is a powerful symbol and a rallying point for unified Indian political activities. It stands out as the site of one of the most significant and successful Indian protest actions of the modern era. More importantly for young Indian people, the occupation of Alcatraz Island was the springboard for the rise of Indian activism that began in 1969 and continued into the late 1970s, as witnessed by the large number of occupations which began shortly after the November 20, 1969, landing. Most scholars, and those who follow Indian issues, recognized that Alcatraz was the true catalyst for the new Indian activism as it became more organized and more "pan-Indian."

The foundation for this and subsequent protest actions was bitter and deep, and had been laid long before the 1969 occupation, however.

Beginning in the 1800s, the United States government pursued a policy—systematic and entrenched—that sought to eradicate American Indian culture, if not the people themselves. What the government and its citizens wanted was land, and they took it, treaties notwithstanding.

WHAT IS IMPORTANT TO US? LAND IS IMPORTANT TO US. WITHOUT LAND, WE'RE NOTHING.

DENNIS BANKS, ANISHINABE

In 1871, Senator Eugene Casserly was quoted as saying "[The Indians'] misfortune is not . . . that they are a dwindling race; nor that they are a weak race. Their misfortune is that they hold great bodies of rich land." The senator's words were apt; since the day the first Europeans set foot on the North American continent, indigenous Americans had fought to retain the territories historically occupied by their respective tribes.

> **THE GOVERNMENT IS NOT HERE TO ENHANCE OUR QUALITY OF LIFE... IT'S HERE TO ELIMINATE US, TO HOMOGENIZE US AND ERASE US.**
>
> JOHN TRUDELL, SIOUX

They battled the French, the Spanish, and the British. Ultimately, however, the new United States of America, with its land hunger, could not be stopped. As Judith Nies points out in her book, *Native American History*, the dawning of the 19th century saw "more than 80 percent of what is now the continental United States [exclusive of the eastern seaboard] in Indian hands. . . . By 1900, the Indians had lost 95 percent of their 1800 holdings."

IN 1935, MY FATHER PASSED AWAY AND MOST OF US [KIDS] WERE SHIPPED OFF TO THE INDIAN BOARDING SCHOOL AT PIPESTONE, MINNESOTA. I GOT TO GO HOME ONCE EVERY TWO YEARS DURING MY STAY AT THE BOARDING SCHOOL, FROM 1935 TO 1945. WHEN I FIRST WENT THERE, I WAS ONLY FIVE YEARS OLD. LIKE MOST INDIAN BOARDING SCHOOLS OF THOSE TIMES, IT WAS REALLY EDUCATION FOR CULTURAL CHANGE.

ADAM FORTUNATE EAGLE, RED LAKE CHIPPEWA

THEY WERE ENCOURAGED TO ABANDON THEIR CULTURES AS A WAY OF BECOMING AMERICAN.

JOSEPH MYERS, POMO

Treaties were used as weapons of both property and cultural encroachment. Through treaties, land was transferred from the tribes to the federal government, and missionaries and educators were introduced; the latter were expected to effect the Indians' assimilation into "real" Americans after they had been dispossessed in the name of real estate.

"Indians developed a unique relationship with the federal government. They couldn't vote; they had no elected representatives; they had no voice in the American political system. Yet they had a complicated series of treaties which had status in law," Nies summarizes.

**WITH HOUSE RESOLUTION 108, THE 1953 TERMINATION POLICY, THE GOVERNMENT BASI-
CALLY SAID "WE'RE GOING TO GET OUT OF THE INDIAN BUSINESS." BY 1969, 106 RESER-
VATIONS, RANCHERIAS, AND BANDS OF INDIANS HAD ALREADY BEEN TERMINATED.**

ADAM FORTUNATE EAGLE, RED LAKE CHIPPEWA

From traditional dress to Carlisle Indian School uniforms—three Sioux boys begin the process of assimilation (1883). Left to right: Timber (Chauncey) Yellow Robe, (Henry) Standing Bear, and Wounded (Richard) Yellow Robe.

Assimilation of Indians into mainstream society became the goal of both those bent on further westward expansion and those who considered themselves supporters of the Indian people. Each reasoned that by eliminating reservations and thereby fracturing remaining tribal structures, beliefs, cultures, and religious practices, Indians would be more readily swallowed up by American culture. The Dawes Act of 1887 formalized these beliefs. It broke up the reservation system and assigned parcels to individual Indians; the balance of the land was determined to be "surplus" and was sold.

Almost a century later, in 1953, Congress unanimously passed a resolution that took another 1,362,155 acres of American Indian land and displaced 11,466 individuals. In this subsequent stepped-up relocation drive, the government promised vocational training, financial assistance, job placement programs, and adequate housing for American Indian people who would move to certain large cities, San Francisco among them. They arrived from their rural homes across the country, enticed by the government's promises of a better and more prosperous life than they could build on the reservation. Reality was often dramatically different. Stories of

WE WERE THE STATISTICS. WE WERE THE UNEMPLOYED AND THE DISENFRANCHISED AND WE WERE THE ONES WHO WERE JUST TRYING TO SURVIVE TERMINATION AND RELOCATION.

JOHN TRUDELL, SIOUX

ABOUT EIGHT OF US WENT BY TRAIN FROM KANSAS TO THE BAY AREA. THE BIA PEOPLE
TOLD US THEY WERE GOING TO MEET US AT THE TRAIN STATION, BUT WHEN WE
ARRIVED IN OAKLAND...NOBODY WAS THERE TO MEET US AND WE DIDN'T KNOW WHAT
TO DO. SO WE TOOK A TAXI DOWNTOWN. LUCKILY, THERE WAS SOMEBODY IN THE
OFFICE AND THEY MADE ARRANGEMENTS FOR US TO STAY SOMEWHERE AND TOLD US
TO COME BACK THE NEXT MORNING. WE SAT THERE IN THOSE OFFICES FOR DAYS ON
END WITH NOTHING TO DO, WAITING TO BE SENT OUT ON INTERVIEWS.

MILLIE KETCHESHAWNO, MVSKOKE CREEK

entire families stranded for days in bus stations, waiting for Bureau of Indian Affairs (BIA) counselors who never arrived, were common. Promises of assistance were hollow. Then, financially trapped in unfamiliar urban environments with no marketable skills and often very little English, many of these relocated people gravitated toward poverty-level housing and welfare.

During relocation, officials made no attempt to locate Indian people near one another. As a result, people from sparsely populated rural areas found themselves in a city dense with humanity, customs, ideas, and technology, little of which they understood. Isolated, impoverished, poorly housed, unassisted by the BIA's relocation commission, and heavily discriminated against, many were overcome and returned to their reservations. Among those who remained, disillusionment, resentment, and distrust were high.

WE WERE THE ONES THAT HAD THE
PROBLEMS WITH ALCOHOL OR WE
HAD COME FROM DIVIDED FAMILIES
AND WE HAD JUST COME OUT OF
THE MEAT GRINDER THAT'S CALLED
DEMOCRACY.

JOHN TRUDELL, SIOUX

These relocatees were not the only native people in the city, however. American Indians had been obliged to enter urban life for many years. Boarding school placement and railroad jobs drew some. Many Indian men who had served in the military during World War II chose to remain with their families in the San Francisco area after discharge; others who had taken defense-industry jobs during the war also stayed. By the mid-1960s, an estimated 40,000 Indian people from one hundred tribal groups lived in the Bay Area, most of them employed in menial jobs at low pay.

WE BECAME INCREASINGLY AWARE...THAT THE BIA RELOCATION PROGRAM DROPPED
US OFF IN THE CITY AND ENDED THEIR RELATIONSHIP WITH US.

LaNADA BOYER, SHOSHONE-BANNOCK

BY ABOUT 1962, AN INTERESTING PHENOMENON WAS TAKING PLACE. LITTLE TRIBAL GROUPS WERE STARTING TO COME TOGETHER. THEY HAD COMMON PROBLEMS AND COMMON CONCERNS AND WANTED TO IDENTIFY WITH EACH OTHER.

ADAM FORTUNATE EAGLE, RED LAKE CHIPPEWA

Slowly and by chance, urban American Indian people began to find one another, and by the late 1960s, they had organized numerous social, religious, and political groups in the city and surrounding Bay Area communities. United Native Americans (UNA), established in San Francisco in 1968, sought to unify all persons of Indian blood throughout the Americas and to develop a democratic grass-roots organization. It was from this and similar alliances that activist leaders came. The emerging Red Power movement, advocating Indian right to self-government, was made up largely of American Indian students from the Bay Area, many of them Vietnam veterans. They spoke out against the treatment they received locally as well as at state and federal levels, in cities and on reservations. An article in *Warpath*, the first militant pan-Indian newspaper in the United States (founded in 1968 by UNA president Lehman Brightman, Mvskoke-Sioux), summed up their perspective:

> The "Stoic, Silent Redman" of the past who turned the other cheek to white injustice is dead. (He died of frustration and heartbreak.) And in his place is an angry group of Indians who dare to speak up and voice their dissatisfaction at the world around them. Hate and despair have taken their toll and only action can quiet this smoldering anger that has fused this new Indian movement into being.

THERE WAS NO PREPARATION, NO ORIENTATION. ONE DAY WE'RE IN A VERY ISOLATED RURAL COMMUNITY, AND A FEW DAYS LATER, WE GET OFF THE TRAIN AND WE'RE IN A HOTEL IN THE RED-LIGHT DISTRICT OF SAN FRANCISCO.

WILMA MANKILLER, CHEROKEE

They wanted the right to control their own lives independent of the federal government; they wanted Indian future to be determined by Indian acts and Indian decisions; they wanted assurance that Indian people would not be separated involuntarily from their tribal groups.

I SAW SIGNS THAT SAID "NO INDIANS OR DOGS ALLOWED." I REMEMBER THE BATHROOMS FOR INDIANS ONLY. AND I REMEMBER THE TREATMENT OF PEOPLE TOWARDS US.

LANADA BOYER, SHOSHONE-BANNOCK

Indians picketed the federal office building in San Francisco in March 1969 to protest the lack of educational opportunities and to accuse the Bureau of Indian Affairs of perpetuating ignorance among American Indian people. Urban vocational training, they asserted, had given them ten thousand welders and mechanics but only seven lawyers, four doctors, and two engineers. One month later, the director of the San Francisco Indian Center and a member of the San Francisco Human Rights Commission called a press conference to object to police racism and brutality toward American Indians. American Indian frustration stemming from years of neglect, poverty, discrimination, and BIA paternalism finally attracted the attention of the Washington bureaucracy.

MOST OF THE MEN WERE TRAINED AS WELDERS. AND THE WOMEN AS BEAUTICIANS. ON THE RESERVATION, WE DON'T HAVE STEEL-FRAME BUILDINGS, AND WE USUALLY JUST WASH OUR HAIR WITH SOAPWEED.
BELVA COTTIER, SIOUX

AFTER WE FORMED OUR ORGANIZATION ON CAMPUS, THEN WE STARTED NETWORKING WITH THE OTHERS...THE BLACK ORGANIZATIONS, THE CHICANO ORGANIZATIONS, THE ASIANS...WE FORMED THE THIRD WORLD COALITION...AND WENT ON STRIKE ON CAMPUS AT BERKELEY IN 1968.

LaNada Boyer, Shoshone-Bannock

Three sisters, ca. 1955, Oakland California. The Oakland Intertribal Friendship House was an important resource for East Bay Indian people. (IFH Archives)

Earlier, in 1966, George McGovern, Democratic senator from South Dakota, had introduced a Senate resolution that stressed the need for Indian people to participate in shaping their destiny. In response, President Lyndon Johnson proposed a new goal for the nation's Indian programs, a goal that would stress self-determination, partnership, and self-help. Issuing Executive Order 11399 in 1968, Johnson established the National Council on Indian Opportunity (NCIO). The Nixon administration followed through on this order in early 1969, appointing Vice President Spiro Agnew as chair, and as members, the Secretaries of the Interior; Agriculture; Commerce; Labor; Health, Education, and Welfare; and Housing and Urban Development, and the director of the Office of Economic Opportunity.

In April 1969, the NCIO held a public forum in San Francisco to identify problems of Indian people and to try to find solutions. At the forum, American Indian people spoke out against problems inherent in the system of government and directed against Indians: racism, educational deficits, inferior healthcare, unemployment, poor housing. They pointed out that in the classroom, Indian children's sense of identity and personal worth were damaged by false and misleading statements in textbooks. The need for culturally relevant courses and Indian studies programs permeated the testimony, as did the lack of opportunity for upward mobility for relocated Indian people. Other testimony concentrated on the difficulties experienced by Indian people in adjusting to urban life.

Signals of rising activism came from Indian political and social organizations. When LaDonna Harris, Comanche, chair of the Committee on Indian Affairs, was asked by the press, "Are you going to have some militant Indians?" she replied, "Heavens, I hope we will." Richard McKenzie, Sioux, said he believed that kneel-ins, sit-ins, sleep-ins, eat-ins, pray-ins "wouldn't help us. We would have to occupy government buildings before things would change."

McKenzie's comment was prophetic. Of the thirty-seven people who testified at the April NCIO forum, twenty-five would be among those who would occupy Alcatraz Island seven months later.

THE LANDINGS

March 1964 and November 1969

THERE WAS THE FREE SPEECH MOVEMENT AT BERKELEY AND THAT REALLY HAD A BIG
IMPACT ON ME. WHEN I SAW MARIO SAVIO STANDING ATOP THAT CAR IN SPROUL PLAZA,
I THOUGHT, HERE'S THIS YOUNG MAN, BRAVE ENOUGH TO STAND UP AND SAY THAT
SOMETIMES YOU HAVE TO STOP THE MACHINERY AND LAY YOUR BODY ACROSS IT IN
ORDER TO MAKE PEOPLE TAKE HEED. YOU HAVE TO STOP THE MACHINERY AND LISTEN.

MILLIE KETCHESHAWNO, MVSKOKE CREEK

THE TEMPER OF SOCIAL CHANGE suffused the entire country during the 1960s as cause-driven crowds poured into the streets, willing to suffer the violence that erupted when police tried to clear them. University and college campuses, particularly in the San Francisco Bay Area, boiled with protests and demonstrations—for civil rights, against the Vietnam War, and against existing systems in general. The frustrations of the Bay Area Indian community had reached a critical juncture in concert with the national consciousness.

AND THE HIPPIES ARE JINGLING, JANGLING, BLOWING SMOKE ALL OVER HAIGHT
ASHBURY, AND THEY WERE LETTING THEIR HAIR GROW LONG. TO THE MALE INDIAN,
THIS WAS A PHENOMENON, BECAUSE FOR AN INDIAN TO GROW HIS HAIR LONG WAS A
VIOLATION OF FEDERAL POLICY OF 1906. ACCORDING TO THE 1906 POLICY, FOOD WAS
WITHHELD UNTIL COMPLIANCE—IN OTHER WORDS [BY TERMS OF THIS POLICY], WE
[COULD] BE STARVED TO DEATH UNTIL WE CUT OUR HAIR.

ADAM FORTUNATE EAGLE, RED LAKE CHIPPEWA

WHEN I WENT TO UCLA, THERE WAS A
VOLATILE MIXTURE OF POLITICS
AND LEARNING OF INDIAN HISTORY.
MANY OF OUR STUDENTS WERE
CLEARLY SHOCKED.

ED CASTILLO, CAHUILLA-LUISEÑO

By 1964, the federal prison on Alcatraz had been closed and the island classified as surplus federal land. In March of that year, five Sioux Indians boarded a chartered boat, landed on Alcatraz, and claimed the island under an 1868 Sioux treaty which entitled them to take possession of surplus land. They signed a formal claim statement to be filed with the Bureau of Land Claims in Sacramento, held a victory dance, and on the advice of their lawyer, Elliott Leighton, left the island. In April, Leighton filed a petition with the General Services Administration (GSA) citing the 1868 treaty as their authority. The Sioux offered to pay 47 cents per acre for the land, the price the government had

Alcatraz dock, 1969; existing signs were quickly altered by the occupiers. (M. Vignes)

WE WENT TO THE BANCROFT LIBRARY IN BERKELEY AND THAT'S WHERE WE FOUND THE BOOK ON PUBLIC DOMAIN LAND. WE MADE COPIES — IT TOOK TWO DOLLARS, WHICH WE BARELY HAD — OF THE SIOUX TREATY. WE STUDIED IT, JUST LIKE LAWYERS, TO SEE IF THEY MEANT WHAT THEY SAID.

BELVA COTTIER, SIOUX

offered for 65 million acres taken from California Native Americans under the Indian Claims Commission Act of 1946.

A presidential commission held hearings on April 24 and 25, 1964, to study uses for Alcatraz. The American Indian Foundation submitted a proposal that called for the island to be the site of an Indian cultural center and university, but the commission ignored the proposal in favor of others. Between 1965 and 1968, the commission introduced bills in both the House and Senate to implement commission recommendations; however, the bills were not acted upon.

WE PICKETED...WE TOLD THEM THAT THEY JUST DROPPED US OFF HERE AND WOULD NOT RECOGNIZE THAT WE HAD TREATY RIGHTS.

LaNADA BOYER, SHOSHONE-BANNOCK

The commission's failure to accept their proposal added to the growing anxiety of Bay Area Indian people, and Alcatraz Island became an icon, representing the many broken treaties and disdain for their goals or needs. Adam Fortunate Eagle, then known as Adam Nordwall, observed:

Every time you crossed the Golden Gate Bridge or the Bay Bridge, you saw that little spot in the water and remembered. Even at night the revolving search-light...beckoned to you. And you thought: Those twenty acres and all those buildings, all empty, falling apart from neglect. And we have nothing.

NOW WE'RE OUT HERE IN THE GREAT DUMPING GROUNDS OF THE CITY. ALL OF THIS ANXIETY AND FRUSTRATION AND BITTERNESS WAS SHAPING UP, BECAUSE THE INDIANS FOUND OUT THAT THEY WERE BEING TRICKED. ON OCTOBER 9, 1969, THE INDIAN CENTER BURNED DOWN.

ADAM FORTUNATE EAGLE, RED LAKE CHIPPEWA

Fortunate Eagle and the Bay Area United Indian Council saw Alcatraz as a symbol powerful enough to bring together the urban Indian community and reach out to those on reservations as well. They defined practical, historical, and political reasons for the island to be turned over to Indian people, and began to draw explicit plans for its use, which included Indian spiritual and ecology centers, a museum, and a training school.

Alcatraz dock area, site of all of the landings. (M. Vignes)

On September 29, 1969, however, before the United Indian Council submitted their formal application, the San Francisco Board of Supervisors endorsed oil baron Lamar Hunt's bid for commercial redevelopment of Alcatraz Island. Hunt's plans included a park commemorating the U.S. space program, illuminated gardens, an underground museum, restoration of the prison for tours, and construction of a shopping center that would recreate 1890s San Francisco. The subsequent public outcry was so great that in October, the GSA gave the Department of the Interior until the first of December to explore federal recreational uses for the site. American Indian students resolved to hold a demonstration on Alcatraz to emphasize their neglected educational needs.

IT WAS LIKE WE WERE AN INVISIBLE PEOPLE. THEY RECOGNIZED EVERYONE ELSE, BUT THEY NEVER RECOGNIZED THE INDIAN PEOPLE — IT WAS LIKE WE WERE PART OF A MUSEUM.

LaNada Boyer, Shoshone-Bannock

ON THE RESERVATION, WE ARE POLITICAL PRISONERS AND DO NOT HAVE RIGHTS AS ANY OTHER AMERICAN. SO WHEN WE'RE HERE IN THE CITY AND WHEN WE THOUGHT ABOUT THE GOVERNMENT ONCE AGAIN NOT RECOGNIZING FEDERAL LAW, NOT RECOGNIZING OUR TREATIES, THAT WAS IT. WE WERE GOING TO TAKE THE ISLAND.

LaNada Boyer, Shoshone-Bannock

On October 10, the San Francisco Indian Center burned to the ground. It had been a meeting place that served some 30,000 Indian people with social programs and provided assistance with employment, health care, and legal matters. The tragic loss of this important facility focused Indian attention on Alcatraz and coalesced groups interested in its use.

Two vital elements now existed: American Indian organizations who had plans for development on Alcatraz, and committed activist American Indian young people (primarily students) who could tolerate hardship conditions on a cold and isolated island for a prolonged period. Within the United Indian Council, planning for a November 9, 1969, occupation of the island moved forward at a quickened pace.

> ## IT'S MY RECOLLECTION...[THAT THE] TWO EVENTS AND TWO ISSUES CONVERGED, THE INDIAN CENTER AND ALCATRAZ.
>
> TIM FINDLEY

Occupation planners, resolved that the movement would promote all American Indian people rather than one tribal group, chose to call themselves Indians of All Tribes. They drew up a proclamation that, though laced with sarcasm, reflected their serious intentions and hope for the future of Indian people:

To the Great White Father and All His People:

We, the native Americans, re-claim the land known as Alcatraz Island in the name of all American Indians by right of discovery.

We wish to be fair and honorable in our dealings with the Caucasian inhabitants of this land, and hereby offer the following treaty:

We will purchase said Alcatraz Island for twenty-four dollars ($24) in glass beads and red cloth, a precedent set by the white man's purchase of a similar island about 300 years ago. We know that $24 in trade goods for these sixteen acres is more than was paid when Manhattan Island was sold, but land values have risen over the years. Our offer of $1.24 per acre is greater than the 47 cents per acre the white men are now paying the California Indians for their land.

We will give the inhabitants of this land a portion of that land for their own, to be held in trust by the American Indian Government—for as long as the sun shall rise and the rivers go down to the sea—to be administered by the Bureau of Caucasian Affairs (BCA). We will further guide the inhabitants in the proper way of living. We will offer them our religion, our education, our life-ways, in order to help them achieve our level of civilization and thus raise them and all their white brothers up from their savage and unhappy state. We offer this treaty in good faith and wish to be fair and honorable in our dealings with the white men.

The proclamation went on to note the similarities between Alcatraz and Indian reservations: isolation from modern facilities, inadequate transportation, no fresh or running water, poor sanitation, no oil or mineral rights, no industry,

high unemployment, no health-care facilities, rocky and non-productive soil, land that does not support game, no schools, and a population held prisoner and kept dependent upon others. A third segment of the proclamation set forth that the site would be used for cultural, ecological and spiritual centers; a training school; and a museum.

An occupation force of seventy-five people arrived at San Francisco's Pier Thirty-nine at ten o'clock on the morning of November 9. None of the five boats Fortunate Eagle had arranged for showed up. The press, however, was present. Fortunate Eagle asked the Indian student groups, now growing in numbers, to keep the media occupied while he secured alternate transportation. Richard Oakes, Mohawk, asked Fortunate Eagle for a copy of the proclamation and permission to read it to the

IT WAS THE FIRST TIME I'D SEEN NATIVE PEOPLE WILLING TO...SAY THIS IS OUR LAND AND WE'RE GOING TO STAND UP FOR WHAT WE BELIEVE IS RIGHT. WE'RE GOING TO TAKE CONTROL OF OUR OWN LIVES.

WILMA MANKILLER, CHEROKEE

> **CHILDREN AND ELDERS [HAD] TO STAY BEHIND. THIS OLD LAKOTA COUPLE...FELT SUCH AN OVERWHELMING GRIEF—THEIR GRANDPARENTS HAD BEEN AT WOUNDED KNEE IN 1890. THEY'D BEEN IN A TEEPEE WHEN THE BULLETS OF THE 7TH, 11TH, AND 14TH CAVALRY CAME SLAMMING THROUGH THE BUFFALO HIDE.**
>
> ADAM FORTUNATE EAGLE, RED LAKE CHIPPEWA

media. An impromptu press conference, formally announcing the occupation, resulted. In the eyes of the media, Oakes became the leader, or at the very least the spokesperson, for the occupying force. To attract media coverage and stall for time, the demonstrators danced and sang.

The owner and skipper of a three-masted sailing ship, the *Monte Cristo*, agreed to provide transportation under certain conditions. They must have Coast Guard permission, only fifty people could board the ship, and they would circle the island rather than risk an attempt to dock. They reached an agreement and cast off.

> **THEY REALLY, REALLY LOVED RICHARD OAKES. HE LOOKED JUST LIKE A BORN INDIAN LEADER. WHERE'D HE COME FROM? I DON'T KNOW, BUT HE HAD ALL THE QUALITIES OF LEADERSHIP.**
>
> JOSEPH MORRIS, BLACKFOOT

As the ship drew within 250 yards of the island, Oakes, not content to make a symbolic claim, shouted "Come on. Let's go! Let's get it on!" and jumped overboard. Jim Vaughn, Cherokee; Joe Bill, Eskimo; Ross Harden, Winnebago, and Jerry Hatch followed. Oakes later related that "I was exhausted when I hit land. I've done a lot of swimming, but this was the toughest swim I've ever made." The *Monte Cristo* and its remaining passengers returned to San Francisco.

When the swimmers reached the island, they were confronted by caretaker Glenn Dodson and his dog; Dodson told

> **THEY WERE YOUNG, THEY WERE BRAVE, THEY WERE WARRIORS, BOTH MEN AND WOMEN.**
>
> STEVE TALBOT

the group that they had to leave. The five young men (Property Management Disposal Service records erroneously showed that there were four) made shore about 4:30 PM, claimed the island by right of discovery, and after a brief time were transported back to the mainland by the Coast Guard.

The remainder of the occupation force decided to make another landing attempt later that day. Participants' memories of the events vary somewhat, but the consensus seems to be that around 6 PM, about twenty people boarded a fishing boat—some say it was the *New Vera* II—and set out. As the boat reached the island, the swirling tide made it extremely dangerous for the captain to tie up to the floating dock. Finally, the boat was secured and people began throwing sleeping bags and other equipment onto the dock. The captain (who had agreed to take the group out for a $3 per person charge but was not aware that they were going to attempt an actual occupation) suddenly realized that he might be an accessory to the trespass of a federal facility. He untied the line, threw the boat's gears into reverse, and pulled away from the dock, leaving part of the occupation force on the island. The fourteen who landed that night included: Jim Vaughn; John Martel, Cherokee; John White Fox, Shosone; John Vigil; Joe Bill;

> ## WE GOT OUT TO THE ISLAND, AND IT WAS A BEAUTIFUL NIGHT, AND IT WAS SO EXCITING. THE COAST GUARD ARRIVED AND CAME OUT WITH THEIR SPOT LIGHTS, BUT THEY COULDN'T FIND US. THEY'D COME SO CLOSE AND YOU'D BE TRYING TO KEEP BACK YOUR LAUGHTER. WE FELT LIKE SUCH — WE *WERE* SUCH KIDS.
>
> LaNada Boyer, Shoshone-Bannock

LaNada Boyer, Shoshone-Bannock; David Leach, Colville-Sioux; Richard Oakes; Bernel Blindman, Sioux; Rich Evening, Shoshone; Fred Shelton, Eskimo; Linda Aranaydo, Creek; Kay Many Horses, Sioux; and Ross Harden. When they reached the island's crest, they saw the sweep of Coast Guard searchlights and knew their mainland compatriots had notified the press of the landing, as prearranged.

On the island, GSA security officer John Hart was immediately aware of this second landing and contacted the GSA to confirm it, although he did not know how many people had landed. He was advised that U.S. marshals had been called and was told to await further instructions.

ALL OF THAT WAS SPONTANEOUS. NONE OF THAT STUFF WAS PLANNED. THEN AS WE GOT CLOSE TO THE ISLAND, SOME OF THE STUDENTS GOT EXCITED. RICHARD OAKES JUMPED OVER THE SIDE, BEGAN TO SWIM ASHORE.

Don Patterson, Tonkawa

The following morning, November 10, T. E. Hannon, regional director of the GSA, accompanied by other officials, two GSA guards, the GSA attorney, and thirty or forty members of the press, went to Alcatraz. Reporters discovered some of the occupiers in the cellhouse's main cellblock, and advised them that the Coast Guard was at the dock and was giving the occupiers a chance to get off the island peacefully before charging them with trespassing on federal property.

The occupiers came out of hiding. Richard Oakes presented Hannon with a proclamation claiming the island by right of discovery, and announced that this was just the beginning of their protest. They returned peacefully to the mainland and dispersed upon landing. No arrests were made and no charges were filed. One of the group later related, "We felt that. . .we wouldn't be doing the movement any good sitting in jail. Besides, this was just the beginning and there was a lot of planning to do. The most important thing in our minds was the fact that the Indians were getting stepped on and we wanted to make them aware of this."

The occupiers left their mark on this small dock-area structure.

THE OCCUPATION

November 20, 1969

THE OCCUPATION OF ALCATRAZ WAS IN REALITY AN ISSUE OF LAW. THE AMERICAN GOVERNMENT SIGNED 300, 400 TREATIES WITH DIFFERENT NATIVE TRIBES IN THIS COUNTRY. WE WERE TAKING THE LEGAL POSITION...SAYING TO THE AMERICAN GOVERNMENT AND THE AMERICAN PEOPLE THAT YOUR GOVERNMENT MUST OBEY THAT LAW.

JOHN TRUDELL, SIOUX

THE RETURN TO ALCATRAZ was not long in coming. Immediately after the November 9 landing, Richard Oakes traveled to the University of California at Los Angeles to recruit additional American Indian students for a prolonged occupation. He spoke to them of the sacrifice and hardship that would come with living on the island and what the act would mean to all Indian people. Eighty students committed to participate in the forthcoming occupation.

Before dawn on November 20, 1969, American Indian people once again sailed to Alcatraz Island. This landing force of seventy-nine consisted of college students, married couples, and six children. Despite their numbers, the group managed to reach the island almost unnoticed by the authorities — once they were there, however, their presence quickly became public knowledge.

Simultaneous with the landing events, Indian activist Adam Fortunate Eagle was in Minneapolis attending the first National Conference on Indian Education. His wife notified him the moment the landing was made, and he asked the conference chairman to recognize him.

WAS THIS A PRANK? WAS THIS A PEOPLE'S PARK KIND OF DEMONSTRATION? DID IT ALL END TOMORROW AND WE GET OUR NAMES IN THE PAPER, OR WILL THIS GO ON FOR A LONG TIME?

BELVA COTTIER, LAKOTA SIOUX

He went before the gathering of Indian scholars, educators, and community leaders to explain the purposes of the occupation and asked them to take copies of the proclamation to share with their tribes. He said, "The response was incredible. All over that big auditorium was cheering as I ended my request....The conference transformed our remote little Indian activity into a national movement with national support."

A juxtaposition of symbols on the cellhouse: the U.S. government's eagle and Apache chief Geronimo, icon of Indian resistance.

On Alcatraz, caretaker Dodson, who said he was one-eighth Indian himself, advised the group that they were trespassing and then directed them to the island's most comfortable quarters, a three-story frame house, once the warden's residence. There they set up their headquarters. They then set out to reconnoiter the entire island, the cellhouse, walkways, and industry buildings for living quarters and secure places to hide if the government attempted to forcefully remove them. With a victory powwow and ceremonial singing accompanied by a drum, they celebrated their successful landing.

WE WERE CRAMMED IN THERE IN THE BOW AND THE NEXT THING YOU KNOW, WE WERE COMING ACROSS [THE WATER], BOUNCING AND STUFF. I WAS SO AFRAID.

SHIRLEY GUEVARA, MONO

By midday, messages lettered in red paint were appearing everywhere on the island. The water tower read *Peace and Freedom...Welcome...Home of the Free Indian Land*. One prohibitory sign was altered to read *Warning Keep Off Indian Property*. Elsewhere, *You Are Now on Indian Land*.

The occupiers released a statement to the press, reading in part:

We have been in this land for thousands of years. After a hundred years as prisoners of this country, we feel that it is time we were free. We have gone to Alcatraz Island to preserve our dignity and beauty and to assert our position with the new weapons we have come to learn how to use. These weapons are the same ones these invaders of our country used to take what they wanted.

These weapons are the laws and lawyers, and the power of the pen to tell our real story.

But in addition, we now have a more powerful weapon. The people of this country know a little of the real history and tragedy of the Indian people. What they do not know is the tragic story of the Indian people today. We intend to tell them that story. This is only the first stepping-stone of a great ladder of Indian progress.

We appeal to your sense of fair play and your desire to do what is right by all peoples. Indian people appeal to you to stand by us and help us in our hour of need.

When John Hart returned to the island from a fishing trip, he found the Indians set up and singing in the warden's residence. A small blaze crackled in the fireplace, and above the mantle, a poster of glowering Apache chief Geronimo watched over the occupants. Sandwiches, potato salad, and soft drinks were laid out on a table. "Well, as long as you're here, you might as well be comfortable," Hart told the group. He pointed out the accessible buildings with working plumbing and warned of hazards on the crumbling catwalks and overgrown stairways of the deteriorating prison.

The Coast Guard established a blockade around the island to prevent the arrival of additional occupiers. In the late afternoon of November 20, GSA regional administrator Hannon; Aubrey Grossman and R. Corbin Houchins, attorneys representing the Indian occupiers; and a Department of the Interior representative arrived. Hannon delivered an ultimatum: the occupiers had until noon the following day to leave; one food supply boat would be allowed through the blockade and any others would be impounded.

As the November 21 deadline passed, it became clear that the Indian occupiers would resist removal. Houchins and Oakes telephoned a message to the Department of the Interior in San Francisco:

> To the Government of the United States from Alcatraz Island, Indian Territory.
> We native peoples of North America have gathered here to claim our traditional and natural right to create a meaningful use for our Great Spirit's land. Therefore, let it be known that our stand for self-determination is on Alcatraz. We invite the United States to acknowledge the justice of our claim. The choice now lies with the leaders of the American Government—to use violence upon us as before to remove us from our Great Spirit's land, or to institute a real change in its dealing with the American Indian. We do not fear your threat to charge us with crimes on our land. We and all other oppressed peoples would welcome spectacle of proof before the world of your title by genocide. Nevertheless, we seek peace.

They concluded with a list of demands that must be met before they would negotiate. The list included requirements that Secretary of the Interior Walter Hickel come to Alcatraz to negotiate; the return of all interests in Alcatraz to American Indians, to be controlled by Indian people without any participation by any agency of the United States government; funding sufficient to build, maintain, and operate an Indian cultural complex and a major university, also to be managed without participation of any federal agency; and no interference with supply of provisions for persons on Alcatraz.

In a press release, they called for support in the form of non-perishable food supplies, which could be dropped off at the temporary American Indian Center, and money to buy building supplies.

IT WAS A WONDERFUL FEELING WHEN WE ARRIVED. WE GOT OFF THE BOAT AND WE WERE ALL THERE TOGETHER AS A UNITED GROUP. WE WERE GOING TO MAKE A STAND AND WE WERE DOING IT ON BEHALF OF OUR PEOPLE.

LaNada Boyer, Shoshone-Bannock

Hickel responded to the proclamation in a press statement, saying he would negotiate at any time but that the demands as set forth were unacceptable. He pointed out that it was not in his power to transfer ownership of the island, and hoped that the Indians would leave for safety's sake. He requested that the GSA do nothing to remove the Indians until after 3 PM on November 23. The GSA honored his request for this cooling-off period.

The Coast Guard blockade, however, was still in effect, making the delivery of supplies by water difficult. A hot-air balloon attempted to get a load of goods in on November 23, but adverse wind conditions prevented its landing. Joe Bill slipped his canoe into the waters and paddled to San Francisco, where he requested donations. That night, a mercy ship came to the Golden Gate side of the island, and while occupiers on the opposite side diverted the attention of the Coast Guard by throwing firebombs at shoreline rocks, others carried supplies up a makeshift ladder laid against the precipitous cliff.

BUD [CROGE] AND JEFF [SHEPHERD] [LIAISONS WITH THE DEPARTMENT OF JUSTICE] SAW THIS AS A LAW ENFORCEMENT PROBLEM. THEY WERE RATHER WILLING AND ANXIOUS TO MOVE THE INDIANS OFF. THE OTHER FACTION WAS GARMENT AND MYSELF, WHO WERE VERY MUCH CONCERNED ABOUT POLITICAL, SMALL "P", ASPECTS AND THE SENSITIVITY ASPECTS OF A FORCEFUL, MAYBE A BLOODY, REMOVAL.
BRADLEY PATTERSON

Donors and occupiers quickly teamed to outmaneuver the Coast Guard. In some instances, a boat would sail by and throw supplies onto a barge docked at the island, where a number of Indians stood by to take donations. Then, as the Coast Guard pursued boat one, boat two would come alongside the barge and unload provisions. Not only was the blockade ineffective, it garnered favorable publicity and support for the occupation group. When it was lifted after only four days in operation, volunteered boats transported food and water and shuttled Indians between island and mainland.

Richard Nixon's presidential special counsel Leonard Garment was one of the first officials notified of the occupation. Garment recognized that this was a full-fledged occupation of a vacant federal government facility rather than ordinary trespass. He feared that the GSA, as a show of force and to bring the occupation to a speedy conclusion, would overreact, and that violence would ensue. Such action would certainly inflame anti-government sentiment in the American public. The Nixon presidency was already experiencing a public relations nightmare—the 1968 massacre of Vietnamese civilians by U.S. Army troops at My Lai was just becoming public knowledge and student unrest was at a fever pitch (the May 1970 shooting of college students at Kent State by National Guardsmen would soon add to the administration's problems). These conditions dictated that removal of Alcatraz occupiers would have to proceed with utmost caution and without shedding American Indian blood. Garment issued orders that his office, acting under the direction of President Nixon, would direct the government's Alcatraz policy. He also ordered the GSA and the FBI to cancel any planned removal of Indian people from the island and to coordinate any future actions with the White House staff.

GARMENT TOLD [GSA ADMINISTRATOR ROBERT] KUNZIG, YOU CALL OFF YOUR COPS. I'M GIVING THE INSTRUCTIONS. WE'RE GOING TO SEND A NEGOTIATOR FROM THE WHITE HOUSE OUT THERE. CALL OFF YOUR COPS, WE'RE COUNTERMANDING YOU.
BRADLEY PATTERSON

DAYS OF EXALTATION

November and December 1969

WHEN I GOT OFF THAT BOAT AND GOT ON THAT ISLAND, HERE'S ALL THESE NATIVE PEOPLE. I DIDN'T KNOW ANY OF THEM, BUT YET, I DID. IT WAS LIKE GOING HOME.

JOHN TRUDELL, SIOUX

WHEN WE GOT TO THE ISLAND, IT SEEMS LIKE WE SHOULD HAVE BEEN SCARED OR SOMETHING, BUT WE WEREN'T. THERE WAS JUST INDIANS. WE HAD BEEN LIVING IN THE CITY AND WERE KIND OF ISOLATED AND LOST FROM BEING INDIANS. SO IT WAS GOOD TO SEE ALL THESE PEOPLE AND THAT'S WHAT MADE IT COMFORTABLE.

EDWARD WILLIE, PAIUTE-POMO

ON THE ISLAND, an organizational framework began to emerge. Occupiers set up a seven-member council, with members to be elected every ninety days. The first group elected were Richard Oakes; Al Miller, Seminole; Ross Harden; Ed Castillo, Cahuilla-Luiseño; Bob Nelford, Eskimo; Dennis Turner, Luiseño; and James Vaughn, Cherokee. Women would take their places on subsequent Alcatraz councils, and their voices were strong throughout the duration of the occupation. LaNada Boyer; Stella Leach, Coville-Sioux; and Grace Thorpe, Sac-Fox, were three of the women often mentioned in media accounts, and there were dozens of others whose contributions were equally important.

The council met to determine which of the numerous and varied issues confronting the occupiers should be addressed and to keep residents informed of political strategies, current events, and other issues of concern. The council members also set up committees: public relations,

THE WOMEN PRETTY WELL SELECTED THE LEADERS AND WE WENT AHEAD AND SELECTED RICHARD OAKES TO REPRESENT US. THE PRESS HAD ALREADY SELECTED HIM...SO WE WENT ALONG WITH THAT.

LaNADA BOYER, SHOSHONE-BANNOCK

health, security, education, research and development, ways and means, food supply, transportation, administration. Meetings were held every Friday, more often if needed.

The entire Indian population of the island voted on all major decisions. Even during bitter disputes, the Alcatraz Indians did not abandon this egalitarianism. According to a non-Indian observer, "When behavior did not conform to the egalitarian standards, such persons were said to be acting like white persons. One frequently heard the admonishment to think and act Indian."

Machinery left behind by the Bureau of Prisons became playgrounds for the children.

(I. Hartmann)

In the early days of the occupation, security was a major concern, and that committee was headed by Jerry Hatch, one of the men who made the November 9 landing. Lookouts stationed on all four corners of the cellblock roof provided security day and night. The committee enforced the regulations adopted by the council to insure the protection and privacy of island residents and to keep visitors and residents from venturing into unsafe areas. The regulations also addressed the introduction of alcohol on the island, housing and job assignments, and control of children.

Feeding the occupiers was a pressing issue from the first day. The kitchen and dining area was a place of camaraderie, men and women joking and laughing as they prepared meals. The mess hall was a happy scene, with small groups discussing work details or other island issues.

> ALCATRAZ WAS ALWAYS A COMMUNITY. WHOEVER WAS LIVING ON THE ISLAND ALWAYS HAD A SAY IN WHAT WAS GOING ON THROUGH OUR WEEKLY COUNCIL MEETING OUR GENERAL MEETINGS. THE DIRECTION DID NOT COME FROM THE LEADERSHIP. IT ALWAYS CAME...FROM THE COMMUNITY.
>
> JOHN TRUDELL, SIOUX

The island now had a growing population of adults and children who brought with them various health-care needs and issues, and life on Alcatraz resulted in numerous scrapes, cuts, bumps, and bruises. Stella Leach, a licensed practical nurse, along with a registered nurse and volunteer doctors Robert Brennan and Richard Fine, operated a health clinic.

> THE FIRST KITCHEN WAS IN THE MAIN CELL BLOCK—THERE WAS A USABLE KITCHEN, SO WE WERE COOKING...HUGE POTS OF STEW. SOME OF THE GUYS WERE COOKS IN THE ARMY SO THEY KNEW HOW TO COOK LARGE QUANTITIES. FOOD WAS PREPARED ALL THE TIME BECAUSE THERE WERE SO MANY PEOPLE COMING, BRINGING DONATIONS.
>
> SHIRLEY GUEVARA, MONO

A nursery cared for children whose parents were occupied with other duties. Dagmar Thorpe (granddaughter of Olympic athlete Jim Thorpe), Maria Lavender, and Lu Trudell staffed it, and in time it evolved into a pre-primary program. American Indian stories, singing, painting, and play activities stimulated learning. Peter Blue Cloud, Mohawk, recalled, "It was reassuring to look into this room and see the many children playing, drawing, or being read to. These children were what the occupation was all about. It was for their futures that we had dared defy the government. To look at these children was to envision an Indian tomorrow of great hope."

The cellhouse kitchen provided enough room to store and prepare food. (M. Vignes)

Within about three weeks of the occupation, the Big Rock School for grades one through six, with an initial enrollment of twelve students, opened in the old movie theater and meeting hall of the prison's main cellblock. The curriculum included reading, writing, arithmetic, geography, health, science studies, and Native American history and culture. Parents and others taught tribal history, traditions, and legends specifically for each child.

Many of the adults realized that neither they nor their children possessed skills or knowledge in the preservation of traditional arts and crafts. These skills, normally passed from generation to generation, had largely been lost to urban Indians, who had little or no reservation or tribal contact. In an art school and crafts training center, adults as well as children learned bead and leatherwork, woodcarving, costume decoration, sculpture, dance, and music. Peter Blue Cloud recalled that: "There was a gentle feeling of calm in the room where the young girls sat beading and making things from hides. Older girls and women taught, by showing, the ancient crafts. Voices here were very quiet. Young boys came to this room to watch, and soon they too were making headbands or pouches. There is a very good feeling in working with the hands, your mind free to wonder and to dream."

Media coverage brought sightseers as well as journalists and photographers from around the globe. In order to maintain control over this large number of people, Alcatraz residents set up a public relations office on the island.

In December 1969, "Radio Free Alcatraz" began broadcasts from the island over KPFA-FM in Berkeley. During the daily fifteen-minute programs, with airtime provided by the Pacifica Foundation, station host John Trudell interviewed residents, spoke about Indian culture, reported on national Indian affairs, and provided an ongoing narrative of the Alcatraz occupation to the listening audience. The following month, occupiers began publishing the *Indians of All Tribes Newsletter* and distributed it across the country; it featured occupation history, Indian activist poetry, and other items of interest to Indian people. Four issues were published before high costs forced its discontinuation. On Thanksgiving Day 1969, local restaurateurs donated two hundred dinners. People across the country gave their support; they came from service clubs and out of the woods in Northern California with food and supplies. Joseph Morris, a Blackfoot Indian and member of the local longshoreman's union, acquired space on Pier 40 and, with volunteer labor, turned it into a staging area from which supplies and people were ferried to Alcatraz. As the volume of donations increased, Scientific Analysis Corporation (SAC) provided a new storage facility without charge.

Money came, too, $4,000 in the first week of occupation. Volunteers kept track of donations and deposited the money into a bank account in the name of Indians of All Tribes. From $15,000 donated by rock-and-roll band Creedence Clearwater Revival, leaders purchased a boat (which they named the *Clearwater*) for $9,000 and used the remainder for food. Nationwide, organizations collected funds, and donations, some quite substantial, came from private citizens.

EVERY DAY, I WOULD DO SOMETHING DIFFERENT. WE GOT INTO MAKING GO CARTS, USING LAUNDRY CARTS AND DOLLIES. WE WOULD MAKE THESE LITTLE CARTS AND PUT THEM AT THE TOP OF THE HILL AND GO DOWN, ZIGZAGGING DOWN TO THE DOCK.

EDWARD WILLIE, PAIUTE-POMO

As interest and support for the occupation grew, so did voluntary assistance. An Indian Desk was set up to handle calls and donations. One worker summed up the efforts of the many volunteers who operated the desk: "Every day was hectic but wonderful."

The occupation force experienced a constant augmentation of its numbers as American Indians began to come and go, some deciding to take up residence, some staying only a few hours or overnight, others required by school or work to leave for extended periods. The occupiers sent out a call on November 29 asking every "tribe, band, or nation" across the country to meet with them on December 23 on Alcatraz to "attempt to bring about Indian unity across the country. . .so we can come to a common understanding of our goals and ideals."

While the government pondered the best approach to the fact of the occupation, the population on the island increased and the attitudes of the occupiers began to take on a new dimension. On November 23, 1969, the *San Francisco Chronicle* claimed "the invaders gave the U.S. government two weeks to surrender." Two days later, Oakes raised concerns among federal officials that other occupations might occur when he proclaimed, "Alaska is next, yes, Alaska!"

The occupiers were in constant need of supplies; Richard Oakes (left) helps unload a pickup on the island.

AN INDIAN COULDN'T WALK DOWN THE STREET WITHOUT A TELEVISION OR NEWSPERSON STOPPING HIM AND SAYING, "HEY, WHAT'S GOING ON WITH ALCATRAZ?"

DON PATTERSON, TONKAWA

DECLARATION OF THE RETURN OF INDIAN LAND

HOW DID WE LOSE OUR LAND?

WARS - MASSACRES - FRAUD - OCCUPATION - EXPROPRIATION - FORCED SALES - DIVISION OF TRIBAL LANDS - DEPRIVATION OF WATER - FLOODING.

WHO TOOK IT?

GOVERNMENT - RAILROAD - OIL - MINING - TIMBER COMPANIES - SETTLERS - HOMESTEADERS - ROBBERS.

WHEN ENGLAND RULED OUR RIGHT TO OUR LAND WAS RECOGNIZED BY THE BRITISH CROWN. AFTER THE REVOLUTION, INDIAN TITLE WAS RECOGNIZED BY THE UNITED STATES IN PROCLAMATIONS BY PRESIDENTS, IN TREATIES & IN STATUTES. VAST AREAS OF THE UNITED STATES WERE CEDED BY INDIAN TRIBES TO THE GOVERNMENT. COULD ANYONE BELIEVE THAT ANY INDIAN TRIBE WOULD VOLUNTARILY CEDE THEIR ANCESTRAL LAND MORE PRECIOUS TO THEM THAN LIFE ITSELF, AND THE SOLE SOURCE OF SATISFACTION FOR THEIR SPIRITUAL, RELIGIOUS AND MATERIAL NEEDS? ALMOST BEFORE THESE TREATIES WERE SIGNED THEY WERE BROKEN - IN ORDER TO TAKE STILL MORE LAND. FINALLY WITHIN THE PAST TWO OR THREE DECADES THE GOVERNMENT HAS CONFERRED THE WRONGS DONE TO THE INDIAN PEOPLE. STATUTES HAVE BEEN PASSED CONCERNING ILLEGALITY, UNCONSTITUTIONALITY AND UNCONSCIONABLE BEHAVIOR AND THE COURTS AND THE INDIAN CLAIMS COMMISSION HAVE BEEN AUTHORIZED TO FIND SPECIFICALLY THE TIMES, PLACES AND VICTIMS OF THESE WRONGS.

HOW DOES THE GOVERNMENT PROPOSE TO RIGHT THESE WRONGS?

IN PLACE OF THEIR LAND THE GOVERNMENT OFFERS TO THE INDIAN TRIBES, AND THE INDIAN PEOPLE. MONEY. HOW MUCH MONEY? FOR CALIFORNIA THEY OFFER 47¢ CENTS AN ACRE FOR LAND WHICH, IN SOME AREAS, IS WORTH 5 MILLION TIMES THAT. FOR THE HUNDREDS OF BILLIONS TAKEN FROM OR EARNED BY INDIAN LAND - NOTHING. FOR MORE THAN ONE HUNDRED YEARS THAT INDIANS HAVE BEEN WITHOUT THEIR LAND - NOTHING.

WILL INDIANS ACCEPT MONEY FOR THEIR LAND?

TO THE GOVERNMENT OF THE UNITED STATES THE INDIAN PEOPLE SAY: YOU CANNOT BE RELIEVED FROM YOUR LEGAL AND MORAL OBLIGATIONS, YOUR CONSCIENCE CANNOT BE ASSUAGED, THE HISTORICAL, SPIRITUAL AND MATERIAL NEEDS OF THE INDIAN PEOPLE CANNOT BE SATISFIED - EXCEPT BY WHAT WE DEMAND, AND BY THIS DECLARATION AFFIRM.

THE RETURN OF OUR LAND

UNDER THE WHITEMAN'S LAW WE HAVE THE RIGHT TO THE RETURN OF OUR LAND. WHEN ONE WHITE MAN ILLEGALLY DEPRIVES ANOTHER OF HIS LAND THE WRONGED ONE ALWAYS GETS BACK HIS LAND. AT THIS VERY MOMENT THE GOVERNMENT IS PROMISING THE TAOS INDIANS THAT THEY MAY REJECT THEIR INDIAN CLAIMS COMMISSION CHECKS AND THEIR HISTORIC BLUE LAKE LAND WILL BE RESTORED TO THEM. IT WOULD HAVE BEEN BETTER FOR THE WHITE MAN'S SELF-ESTEEM & WORLD-IMAGE IF HE HAD DONE WHAT WE MUST DO. INDIAN PATIENCE & FORBEARANCE BEING EXHAUSTED, WE CANNOT & WILL NOT WAIT ANY LONGER. FROM THE FACTS, THE LOGIC AND THE VERITIES WE HAVE RECITED, IT FLOWS AS INEVITABLY AND RELENTLESSLY AS THE GREAT RIVERS OF OUR COUNTRY, THAT WE MUST, AND WE DO DECLARE

OUR LAND IS OURS AGAIN

AS A FIRST STEP WE ANNOUNCE, ON BEHALF OF ALL THE INDIAN PEOPLE, OR TRIBES THAT FROM THIS DAY FORWARD WE SHALL EXERCISE DOMINION, AND ALL RIGHTS OF USE AND POSSESSION, OVER ALCATRAZ ISLAND IN SAN FRANCISCO BAY. HENCEFORTH, FROM TIME TO TIME, THE INDIAN PEOPLE, OR TRIBES OR OTHER GROUPINGS OF INDIAN PEOPLE, WILL SIMILARLY ANNOUNCE THE RESTORATION OF OTHER LAND TO INDIAN DOMINION, USE AND POSSESSION.

WHAT WE HAVE DONE BY THIS DECLARATION WE HAVE DONE FOR INDIANS - BUT TO THOSE WHITES WHO DESIRE THEIR GOVERNMENT TO BE A GOVERNMENT OF LAW, JUSTICE AND MORALITY, WE SAY

WE HAVE DONE IT ALSO FOR YOU

INDIANS OF ALL TRIBES, INC.
ALCATRAZ ISLAND
MAY 31ST 1970

BEAR FORGETS

PROPOSALS AND COUNTERPROPOSALS

December 1969 to May 1970

IT WAS A WAIT-IT-OUT SITUATION. BUT WE WERE USED TO THOSE CONDITIONS. WE LIVED THAT WAY ALL OUR LIVES.

SHIRLEY GUEVARA, MONO

ALTHOUGH THE GSA AND FBI had been informed that the Alcatraz situation would be directed from the White House, each agency continued to look internally for solutions. The White House reacted to this continuing leadership confusion by calling a meeting with the presidential staff, the Department of the Interior, the Department of Justice, and the GSA. During the meeting, it was reiterated that White House special counsel Garment had the lead and Hannon would serve as the GSA liaison. Although the FBI should continue to make situation reports, it was not to interfere with the occupation or go to the island.

The occupiers recognized that they could bargain from a position of strength only as long as they physically occupied the island, and they refused to leave peacefully. A GSA news release dated December 1, 1969, maintained that "federal officials will not hold discussions with the Indians on the future of the island as long as they continue to occupy it." Public pressure, newspaper articles, telephone calls, and telegrams to political leaders at all levels of state and federal government, including the president, forced concessions. Though meetings were held on the island, no points of compromise were reached. The occupiers remained fixed in their demands and the government, equally fixed in its refusal. Since force could not be used, isolation, time, and the federal bureaucracy would be allowed to wear them down.

THE GOVERNMENT WAS NEVER GOING TO BUILD A UNIVERSITY ON ALCATRAZ OR GIVE THEM $300,000 FOR A CULTURAL CENTER...OR EVEN GIVE THEM TITLE TO ALCATRAZ.

BRADLEY PATTERSON

In a manner similar to traditional practice, the Indians of All Tribes recorded their demands on a piece of tautly stretched hide. (I. Hartmann)

AND IT DAWNED ON ME THAT WE WERE GOING TO BE OUT HERE, NOT ONLY FOR THANKSGIVING BUT PROBABLY FOR CHRISTMAS AND BEYOND. IT REALLY BEGAN TO STRIKE HOME THAT THE GOVERNMENT WAS NOT GOING TO MOVE US ON.

ED CASTILLO, CAHUILLA-LUISEÑO

On December 13, the National Park Service recommended that Alcatraz be included in a proposed Golden Gate National Recreation Area, and did not mention American Indians occupying the island. On the eighteenth, Senator George Murphy (Democrat, California) proposed that the island be designated Indian National Park, available to all people, with ownership still resting with the national park system. The *San Francisco Examiner* reported on December 24, and White House press secretary Ron Ziegler denied, that the government had offered Fort Miley to the occupiers as an alternate site for their planned facilities. Hannon reported on December 31 that the Alcatraz Indians would consider "offers of other federal properties, but only in addition to Alcatraz." As 1969 and the first month of the occupation came to a close, it was apparent that the government had no intention of granting the occupiers title to the island.

> **PEOPLE ARE SHOWING UP, WANTING TO GET INVOLVED IN THE MOVEMENT. ALL OF A SUDDEN, IT BECAME AN ALCATRAZ THING; ALMOST NOBODY KNEW THAT THE INDIAN CENTER WAS THE PRIMARY FOCUS HERE.**
>
> DON PATTERSON, TONKAWA

On the mainland, other concerns were surfacing. Donald Patterson, president of the American Indian Center, expressed his frustration at trying to rebuild the center after the October 1969 fire: "It will not be easy and . . . Alcatraz, unfortunately, has been of little help to its older mainland counterpart. . . . There is plenty of unity and energy among Bay Area Indians, but contributions are split between the center and Alcatraz."

Day by day, the island became an increasingly difficult place on which to live. On December 4, all power on the island was out, the auxiliary power generators were inoperative, food was spoiling for lack of refrigeration, and the GSA had directed disconnection of incoming telephone lines. And everything seemed to be leaking— the primary water main, the fuel line (which reduced the supply to one day's worth), and steam return lines.

> **THE SAFE ROUTE FOR THE GOVERNMENT TO GO WAS TO GO AHEAD WITH THE IDEA OF THE NATIONAL PARK. PEOPLE HAVE THE JOY AND PLEASURE OF GOING OUT AND SEEING ONE OF AMERICA'S MOST TERRIBLE FEDERAL PRISONS AND A PRISON WHERE INDIANS WERE HELD CAPTIVE BACK IN THE LAST CENTURY, INCLUDING 16 HOPIS. AND WHAT WAS THEIR FEDERAL CRIME? REFUSING TO LET THEIR CHILDREN BE TAKEN AWAY TO BOARDING SCHOOL.**
>
> ADAM FORTUNATE EAGLE, RED LAKE CHIPPEWA

Divergent voices, as well, began to make themselves heard on the island. Some of the seven-member leadership council were resentful of Richard Oakes, who had received a great deal of media attention. Most of the students in the original

WE WERE ALL COLLEGE STU-
DENTS, LITERALLY EVERY ONE
OF US, WITH ONE OR TWO
EXCEPTIONS. WE WERE VERY
IDEALISTIC. THE PEOPLE WHO
CAME AFTER US WERE OLDER,
MORE CYNICAL. SOME HAD
SERIOUS ADDICTION PROBLEMS.
THEY BEGAN CHALLENGING
RICHARD'S LEADERSHIP. THE
CHALLENGES WERE VERBAL
AND PHYSICAL.

ED CASTILLO, CAHUILLO-LUISEÑO

occupation group returned to college in January, and the solidarity shown by those students was compromised by the arrival of Native Americans unaware of Bay Area Indian problems and unwilling to learn about the original motives for the occupation. Recent occupiers saw Oakes as a threat and obstacle to their control of the island. A struggle for leadership distracted the Indian people from their original altruistic vision and concentrated instead on access to power and money. The security force originally formed to protect the island population became an enforcement group that was known to use brutality to influence leadership choices.

WE WERE VERY SURPRISED WHEN THE GOVERNMENT DID NOT REMOVE US IMMEDIATELY BUT WE HAD THE FEELING THAT IT COULD HAPPEN ANY TIME. SO WE JUST LIVED FROM DAY TO DAY AND OVER THE LONG HAUL WE JUST STARTED ORGANIZING OUR DAILY ACTIVITIES.

LaNada Boyer, Shoshone-Bannock

Barely six weeks after the occupation began, tragedy struck. On January 3, 1970, Oakes's thirteen-year-old stepdaughter Yvonne died in a fall as she played with a group of children in an abandoned building. Several versions of how it happened emerged: she was sliding down a banister in the old guard's quarters, she fell from the second-story balcony in the main cellblock, she fell down the steps in the old guard's quarters, she was pushed by some unknown person. The truth of the incident was never determined.

Oakes and his wife Anne suspected that Yvonne's death was not accidental but was the result of jealousy arising out of Oakes's recognition by the press and government negotiators. Oakes requested that the FBI and the San Francisco Coroner's Office investigate to ascertain if there was foul play, but there was insufficient evidence for either agency to determine that her death was other than accidental.

A few days after Yvonne died, Oakes and his family left the island for good. Anne Oakes later told Hannon that she had wanted to leave the island "for some time and the accident settled it." Their other children were being verbally abused and their oldest son had been seriously beaten two weeks prior to Yvonne's fall.

Oakes's resignation from the council and departure from the island created a leadership void. Not only was he instrumental in the development of the occupation concept, he was the unifying force that galvanized student participation. Oakes was also one of the strongest links between island and urban Indian organizations. Once he left Alcatraz, disarray and confusion seemed to gradually engulf the occupiers. The council continued to function, but the focus and direction of the occupation was lost. What had begun as a symbolic action to benefit Indian people of all tribes quickly became a struggle for individual power and self-aggrandizement. The occupiers found themselves free from city, state, and federal control; could come and go as they pleased; answered to no one; and had a large amount of cash for which they did not have to account to any agency. This license would eventually lead to the occupation's downfall.

The government appointed Robert Robertson, acting executive director of the National Council on Indian Opportunity, to serve as their representative in San Francisco, answering through chain of command to White House special counsel Garment. Robertson, accompanied by GSA official Hannon and others, toured the island on January 10, 1970, and met with occupiers the following day "to discuss health and safety hazards." His tour led him to believe that Alcatraz was "a menace to the health and safety of any human being on it," and that it was "only a matter of time before someone else died there." As the meeting continued, issues ranging far afield from health and safety arose. When Indian participants attempted to draw Robertson into a discussion of title to Alcatraz, Hannon provided a brief explanation of federal law governing disposal of excess property, to which the Indians responded that "the government could do whatever it wanted in spite of the law." Hannon attempted to highlight the problems that had caused the federal government to abandon the prison in 1963, noting the "advanced deterioration" of the buildings, and that the "water barge could sink any time now." He estimated that it would take $8 million to restore water, electricity, sanitation, and acceptable safety standards on the island. The Indians felt that if the government could fight a war and render foreign aid, it could give them what they wanted.

> **THEY WERE ALL CHIEFS, EVERY ONE OF THEM.**
>
> JOSEPH MORRIS, BLACKFOOT

INDIAN POLITICS ARE JUST LIKE EVERYBODY ELSE'S POLITICS. THERE WERE A LOT OF DIFFERENT IDEAS ON WHO WAS GOING TO BE IN CHARGE AND WHO WAS GOING TO MAKE THE RULES AND BE EXEMPT FROM THE RULES.

ED CASTILLO, CAHUILLO-LUISEÑO

Robertson proposed that all women and children leave the island immediately and that only a small symbolic force of five to fifteen men stay. When he suggested paying the remaining men to be caretakers, the occupiers accused him of trying to buy them off and expressed fear that the government would arrest a reduced force.

Richard Oakes (right) represented the idealism of the occupation's early days. (M. Vignes)

WE BELIEVE THAT THE FEDERAL GOVERNMENT DID TRY TO ORCHESTRATE DISSEN-
SION...SOME OF [THE LEADERS] WERE TAKEN TO VERY NICE HOTELS, GOT VERY NICE
MEALS. WE KNOW THAT THE OUTSIDE INDIAN COMMUNITY ALSO WAS APPROACHED BY
THE GOVERNMENT...

Ed Castillo, Cahuilla-Luiseño

At the January 10 meeting, Stella Leach, who oversaw the clinic operation, read a list of health and safety items needed: clinic supplies, telephone service for emergency use, transportation for personnel and supplies, docking privileges on the San Francisco mainland, fire-fighting equipment, workers to repair and install utilities. Hannon ignored her requests and instead read a prepared statement asserting that the American Indians were trespassers and that the government assumed no responsibility for their safety while on Alcatraz.

Following the meeting, Robertson informed the vice president and Garment that "reason is a commodity they want nothing to do with—they are emotionally charged, naive, and not used to responsibility. All they want is the island and an unending flow of money to do what they want, whether what they want has any chance of success or not. Their attorneys are good only for throwing fuel on the fire of unreasonableness." Further, he contended that there was no real leadership on Alcatraz because of the pure democracy and the constant jockeying for power among individuals. A *San Francisco Examiner* headline summed up the two-day meeting: Alcatraz Talks Make Little Headway.

A mainland meeting of the regional council and Indian representatives took place on January 15 to find an "accepted representation of Bay Area Indians" to whom a planning grant "formulating their needs" could be made. Hannon observed that "the 50 or so American Indians on Alcatraz appear to have objectives quite different from the 17,000 or so on the mainland in this area.... The required $5 million to demolish the existing hazardous structures and make the terrain safe...does not appear justified.... Sums of this kind could be much better devoted to meeting the problems of housing, education, health, and employment involving large numbers of American Indians in the Bay Area." Upset, some of the invited Indians and observers walked out of the meeting. Robertson remained optimistic and promised to "meet with them as soon as they [organized] their new group and presented concrete proposals." No further progress was made during January, however.

On February 9, 1970, the Indians of Alcatraz issued a press release announcing the formation of a group that would meet with government negotiators. The Bay Area Native American Council (BANAC) represented twenty-six organizations, which in turn represented some 40,000 Indians from more than seventy-eight tribes throughout the United States and Canada. Initially formed in response to comments made at the mid-January meeting, BANAC was to be the "responsible" group of Indian people to which the government could give a grant. The government had high hopes for the organization and as Bradley Patterson noted in a letter, had

John Trudell (center, seated) was the public "voice of the occupation" and took an active role in the negotiations. (M. Vignes)

"encouraged the BANAC group to organize itself and held out the prospect of real financial and other assistance if they could get their act together." At the heart of this assistance was a $50,000 grant to design solutions to the needs of Bay Area urban Indians, including replacement of the San Francisco Indian Center. Although the Nixon White House rejected some of the Alcatraz methods, the purpose of the $50,000 grant was to "demonstrate the government's reasonableness and willingness to work with a group dedicated to improvement of Indian conditions in lawful ways."

Proposals and counterproposals between government negotiators and the occupiers during March, April, and May 1970 effectively brought an end to the possibility of an amicable resolution of the occupation. Indians of All Tribes representatives finally proclaimed that they were willing to negotiate only on "money and the time and the day that they [the federal government] will turn over the deed to this island. That is all that is negotiable."

The leaders of the Alcatraz council believed that the approaching summer would bring a new influx of American Indians to the island as well as more donations. They had survived a harsh winter and looked forward to a summer free of control other than their own. They refused to bargain away their hard-earned position.

Hannon announced on May 27, 1970, that the government would transfer title to the island to the Department of the Interior. On May 28, the government cut off the remaining electrical power and telephone service to the island.

MONTHS OF TURMOIL

May 1970 to June 1971

THE OCCUPATION WAS SLOWING DOWN. PEOPLE WERE NO LONGER COMING BY AS OFTEN TO DROP OFF WATER OR FOOD.

Shirley Guevara, Mono

FOR THE MOVEMENT, lack of accountability for funds became a problem and hurt public support for the occupation. There were accusations that money had been misappropriated and diverted. Later one of the occupiers related, "We had a lot of money coming in, and we just didn't know how to handle everything and some of it got lost. I think that was our downfall."

THE RENT ON [PIER 40] WAS IN MY NAME AND IT WAS ONLY $10 A MONTH. I FIGURED... THEY HAD ALL KINDS OF LOANS, WHY COULDN'T THEY PAY THE RENT? SO THEY WROTE ME A CHECK FOR $70 AND I TOOK IT TO THE FERRY BUILDING. PRETTY SOON, THE PEOPLE AT THE FERRY BUILDING CALLED ME BACK AND SAID, "YOUR CHECK BOUNCED."

Joseph Morris, Blackfoot

Whatever the amount of money donated may have been, it did not remain on the island long. Chartering boat transport and purchasing food and water required considerable financial resources. Because of the need for money, some occupiers stripped copper pipes from bathroom fixtures and from electrical wiring to sell on the mainland as scrap metal. The government became aware of the "scrapping" and arrested and charged some of those involved with stealing and selling 1,665 pounds of copper from the prison.

The fires that razed several historic buildings and the shutdown of the celebrated Alcatraz lighthouse fur-

I THOUGHT WE COULD DEAL WITH THE GOVERNMENT WHEN I FIRST WENT TO ALCATRAZ, THE SAME WAY MY ANCESTORS, WHEN THEY FIRST MET THEM, THOUGHT THEY COULD DEAL WITH THEM.

John Trudell, Sioux

The burned-out lighthouse and warden's house loom over the dock area.

ther damaged the occupiers' image. In late May 1970, the water barge that had supplied the island had been removed by the Coast Guard with the ostensible intent of refilling it and returning it to the island. At the same time, the last of the GSA personnel was removed from the island. On June 1, seventy-five occupiers (men, women, and children) were left without water or power. At about 11 PM, the Coast Guard dispatched a boat to investigate a glow through the fog from Alcatraz and found that the whole east end of the island appeared to be burning. Coast Guard boats approached Indians on the dock, prepared to evacuate them if necessary, and were told that the occupants did not wish to be evacuated. It was noted that no fire-fighting equipment was known to be on the island, and restricted visibility limited any further evaluation. Government officials blamed the fire on the occupiers, and the occupiers charged that a group of whites who slipped past their security after dark had started it.

As early as May 18, 1970, Hannon had requested that the Department of Justice take steps to remove the occupiers, citing the lack of leadership and discipline, the reported widespread use of narcotics and intoxicants, and potential health problems as too serious to ignore. After the fires, government officials began to quietly consider removal options.

IT JUST WENT UP LIKE PAPER. AND THEY COULDN'T PUT IT OUT. THERE WAS NO WATER. I MEAN, PEOPLE ARE SAYING, OH YEAH, THE INDIANS BURNED IT DOWN, BUT YET YOU TAKE OUR BARGE, YOU TURN OFF OUR ELECTRICITY, SO HOW ARE WE SUPPOSED TO PUT IT OUT?

SHIRLEY GUEVARA, MONO

President Richard Nixon began his address to Congress on July 8, 1970, by repudiating the government policy of termination of Indian tribes. He acknowledged the unconscionable plight of American Indians, stating, "The first Americans—the Indians— are the most deprived and most isolated minority group in our nation. On virtually every scale of measurement—employment, income, education, health—the condition of the Indian people ranks at the bottom." The president announced a new policy of "self-determination without termination," declaring, "It is long past

THEY WANTED TO INCORPORATE IT INTO THE PARK SYSTEM. THEY HAD TAKEN OUR WATER. AND THEN THE FIRE HAPPENED. AND IT WILL NEVER BE KNOWN WHO STARTED THE FIRE. IT COULD HAVE BEEN THEIR SIDE, IT COULD HAVE BEEN OUR SIDE, IT COULD HAVE BEEN BOTH SIDES.

JOHN TRUDELL, SIOUX

time that the Indian policies of the federal government began to recognize and build upon the capacities and insights of the Indian people." Government officials hoped that the formal end of the termination policy and other concessions would prove to the occupiers that their voices had been heard and that the Nixon administration was sincere about addressing Indian issues.

Hard on the heels of this show of support for Indian issues, it seemed unwise to force the occupiers to leave. In view of waning public support for the Alcatraz Indians, the government chose to "isolate the Indians and simply leave them alone on Alcatraz, to make their lives there more difficult than it is now" (in the words of Robert Robertson), and thereby further increase the high attrition rate.

THEY GAVE US THEIR WORD...
THAT WE WOULD NOT BE
REMOVED FROM THAT ISLAND,
NO ACTION WOULD BE TAKEN
AGAINST US... WHILE WE WERE
NEGOTIATING. THEY OFFERED
US $250,000 AND THE LEASE
TO HALF THE ISLAND. WE
REJECTED THE [MONEY] AND
THAT'S WHEN THEY MOVED.
FROM THAT POINT ON,
I REALLY UNDERSTOOD
AMERICA'S MORALITY.

JOHN TRUDELL, SIOUX

The actual removal would not be carried out until after public opinion had shifted to the side of the government.

Termination of power to the island had rendered the lighthouse and fog signals inoperable, and concerns arose for navigation safety in the bay. The Coast Guard attempted to restore the navigational aids and were met by island occupants wielding what appeared to be Molotov cocktails. In keeping with the government's policy of avoiding violence, the Coast Guard did not challenge them. Hannon issued a press release on August 8, asserting that the Coast Guard, in response to the genuine need to provide navigational safety, would reactivate the lighthouse and foghorns on the island. These actions were not subject to qualification or negotiation of any kind. He said he felt confident that the people on the island would not wish to endanger maritime safety and would cooperate with the Coast Guard. The Alcatraz group issued their own ultimatum: "No water, no Coast Guard repair crew."

The already-eroding support for the occupiers took a blow when a two-and-one-half-foot-long arrow with a metal tip, fired from the island, struck a crowded harbor excursion boat. Three days later, someone hurled a Molotov cocktail from the island in the direction of a Coast Guard boat servicing temporary buoy fog signals. Rather than simply occupying an isolated vacant government facility, the Alcatraz Indians were now perceived as endangering civilian and military personnel.

In late August 1970, California governor Ronald Reagan announced the approval of the $50,000 planning grant to BANAC for programs that would

address the needs of urban Indians in the Bay area, but that would not be used to support the people on Alcatraz Island. The Indian people, particularly those on Alcatraz, considered the grant an attempt to drive a wedge between the urban Indian population and the occupiers. Government officials had indeed begun to focus on circumventing the island movement by funneling money into a mainland cultural center, shifting attention to the support of a representative group of Bay Area Indians, and refusing to meet with the Indians on Alcatraz. BANAC's first move was to cease talks: "BANAC will go on record as supporting the Alcatraz movement by suspending any negotiations with other Indian organizations in the Bay Area now in progress with the federal government until the government recognizes the Alcatraz budget and their program proposal is funded."

> THIS WAS A SYMBOLIC GESTURE, A RATHER IMPORTANT, VERY VISIBLE SYMBOLIC GESTURE AND WE WERE QUITE SYMPATHETIC TO THIS AND THAT WAS ANOTHER REASON WHY WE DID NOT WANT TO DO SOMETHING STUPID LIKE USE EXCESSIVE FORCE TO REMOVE THE OCCUPIERS.
>
> BRADLEY PATTERSON

Finally, in mid-August 1970, the government began to formulate plans to restore the lighthouse beacon and foghorns on the island, and, under the code name "Operation Parks," to remove the occupiers. Two private citizens in high-rise apartment buildings on the mainland conducted surveillance and provided daily reports of arrivals and departures from the island. When the population was at its lowest, the Coast Guard would make another attempt to reactivate the aids to navigation. If they were not allowed on the island, United States marshals would take over and evict the occupiers, and GSA guards would secure the land. Information was leaked to Herb Caen, a columnist for the *San Francisco Chronicle*, who forewarned the occupiers in his column. Orders to activate "Operation Parks" were never issued.

The occupiers celebrated the one-year anniversary of the occupation by unveiling plans for a $6 million, tuition-free Indian college on the island, one that would offer courses in Indian arts and crafts, laws, ecology, and languages. It was clear that the occupiers were still adamant about the construction of a university and were not going to leave voluntarily. Of the original occupiers, only LaNada Boyer and John White Fox remained.

In mid-January 1971, two supertankers collided near the Golden Gate Bridge, dumping approximately 800,000 gallons of crude oil into the ocean and causing public support for the island occupiers to decrease even further. A *San Francisco Chronicle* editorial, while acknowledging that the absence of navigational aids had nothing to do with the collision, stated that it was a "sad but incontestable fact that the Indians who have seized the island had completely inactivated its navigational aids and made it a rocky peril in the middle of the bay." The editorial called for the Indians of Alcatraz to reactivate the diaphones and light in order to guard against future accidents and to save the bay and the environment.

The Indians of Alcatraz did little to improve their position with government negotiators or to resolve the growing rift between themselves and the larger Bay Area Indian community. While rumors increased regarding the lawlessness on the island, BANAC met twice with the occupiers to negotiate an amicable solution. A letter from LaNada Boyer dispelled any hopes of the occupiers becoming more tractable:

> The whole action of taking the island was symbolic of telling the American Government and American people that they are not going to continue to steal our lands nor were they going to tell us what to do....We cannot let Alcatraz die.... It will be symbolic of our death if it should die....We need title to have complete and permanent victory.

A *San Francisco Chronicle* article summed up the frustration of the Indians on the island and those on the mainland, and of the government negotiators:

> A band of 20 to 30 Indians still sits defiantly on Alcatraz Island, a bitter, disorganized remnant of the original invaders.
>
> What to do about them...is a question which equally frustrates the federal government and mainland Indian leaders. Government officials indicate some sort of unwanted show-down may be forthcoming and express hope that nobody gets hurt in the process.
>
> "The purpose of occupying Alcatraz was to start an Indian movement and call attention to Indian problems," says Adam Fortunate Eagle..."It has served its purpose. Look at the gains Indians have made since. I don't want to say Alcatraz is done with, but no organized Indian groups are active there. It has turned from an Indian movement to a personality thing. When we occupied the island, we caught the government, and then our occupation forces caught us."

In mid-April, government officials made one last attempt to negotiate with the island council to allow for "face-to-face" discussions without the press, tape recorders, or cameras. John Trudell opened the session by reiterating that the occupiers wanted title to the island. He said the group was willing to make concessions regarding federal jurisdiction over the island but had been offered nothing in return.

When asked if the Indians would settle for land on the mainland to start a school instead of title to Alcatraz, Trudell refused. That was the final straw.

Conditions on the island continued to worsen. On April 19, the *Clearwater*, the main link to the mainland, sank at its moorings. With no funds to purchase or rent transportation, the occupiers were virtually confined to the island with no fresh water, electrical power supplied by a few overloaded gas-powered generators, and only a small amount of food.

June 11, 1971: Armed federal agents arrive to remove the fifteen individuals still on the island.

WE COULDN'T GET BACK. THIS WAS OUR HOME, AND WE COULDN'T GET BACK.

SHIRLEY GUEVARA, MONO

The government once again waited to see if the occupiers would voluntarily leave, but at the end of ninety days, its patience had been tried to the fullest. The island population was thought to be between eleven and fifteen. Trudell and other occupiers were traveling across the country to solicit donations and reinforcement personnel. If the government was going to remove the people from Alcatraz without a major engagement, it would have to be before a summer influx of people and goods.

On June 11, 1971, U.S. marshals; GSA security personnel; and FBI agents armed with revolvers, M-1 carbines, shotguns, and radio transceivers landed from three Coast Guard vessels and a helicopter. The fifteen remaining occupiers—six men, four women, and five children—offered no resistance, and in less than thirty minutes the occupation that had lasted nineteen months and nine days was over. Upon hearing of the removal, Richard Oakes called the government's action "a sissy victory" and compared it to failures in Vietnam.

When the media visited the site two days later, they reported that it was "more like an autopsy" than a tour, a vista of squalor, filth, systematic pilfering, and

mindless destruction. Tom Scott, PMDS realty officer, expressed the sentiments of many observers when he commented that he "had a great deal of respect for Richard Oakes and some of the others who began this. . . .At first, they were so excited, charged up with a real cause. Later they didn't seem to know what the cause was or why they were here."

Alcatraz Island passed into the hands of the National Park Service in October 1972 and became a part of the Golden Gate National Recreation Area.

EPILOGUE: Alcatraz After the Occupation
Between the time the occupiers were removed in June 1971 and the island became a National Park Service site in October 1972, it continued to be administered by the General Services Administration (GSA). So that no other group would be tempted to occupy the island, the GSA demolished the residential complex on the former parade ground. Indeed, it was this destruction that galvanized people in the Bay Area to call for the island's inclusion in the proposed urban national park. Since Alcatraz was opened to the public in 1973, National Park Service planning and preservation efforts have been directed at the protection and interpretation of the island's man-made and natural features—at telling all of the island's stories for the benefit of this and future generations.

IT WAS WITH A GREAT DEAL OF SADNESS THAT WE SAW THE END OF THE OCCUPATION, BECAUSE IT WAS THE BREAKING UP, ESSENTIALLY, OF WHAT HAD BECOME A COMMUNITY, AN INTERTRIBAL COMMUNITY, THERE.

WILMA MANKILLER, CHEROKEE

THE IMPACT

ALCATRAZ ENCOURAGED YOUNG PEOPLE TO BECOME THEMSELVES, AS OPPOSED TO HIDING THEIR INDIANNESS. I REALLY THINK THAT KIND OF INSTITUTIONAL PATERNALISM OR RACISM...AFFECTED INDIAN PEOPLE. ALCATRAZ CHANGED [THINGS].

JOSEPH MYERS, POMO

AS A RESULT OF THE OCCUPATION, either directly or indirectly, the federal government ended its official policy of termination of Indian tribes and adopted a policy of Indian self-determination. In 1970, the administration introduced twenty-two legislative proposals on behalf of American Indians to support tribal self-rule, foster cultural survival as a distinct people, and encourage and support economic development on reservations. Six were passed into law that year, and forty-six the following year. Public laws established within the Department of the Interior the position of assistant secretary of Indian affairs, and established Navajo Community College on the Navajo Reservation and the Native Alaska Claims Act. The life of the Indian Claims Commission was also extended. A large number of these laws returned land or awarded judgment funds as a result of commission's decisions.

In addition to the new legislation, President Nixon increased the BIA budget by 225 percent, doubled funds for Indian health care, established the Office of Indian Water Rights, and made special provisions for defending Indian natural resource rights in federal court. New bureaus were created in each of the government's human-resource departments to help coordinate and accelerate programs for American Indians. Education efforts were expanded, with an increase of $848,000 in scholarships for Indian college students. The Office of Equal Opportunity doubled its funds for Indian economic development; tripled its expenditures for alcoholism and other recovery programs; and significantly expanded programs in housing, home improvement, health care, emergency food, legal services, and education.

I BELIEVE IT WAS THE BEGINNING OF THE PAN-INDIAN MOVEMENT IN THE UNITED STATES.

ED CASTILLO, CAHUILLA-LUISEÑO

In December 1970, Pueblo religious leader Juan de Jesus Romero, 90, watched as President Richard Nixon signed the bill that gave Taos Pueblo title to its sacred Blue Lake.

The occupation lives on today among American Indian People and remains a powerful tribute to united Indian activism. On Thanksgiving Day of each year since 1969, Indian people have gathered on Alcatraz Island to honor those who participated in the occupation and those who today are carrying on the struggle for Indian rights. On February 11, 1978, Indian participants began the "Longest Walk" to Washington, D.C., in protest of the government's continuing ill-treatment of Indian people; the walk began on Alcatraz Island. On February 11, 1994, American Indian Movement leaders undertook a nationwide "Walk for Justice." That walk, too, began on Alcatraz.

BEFORE ALCATRAZ, I HAD NO IDEA WHAT AN INDIAN WAS. PEOPLE WOULD ASK ME, "ARE YOU INDIAN?" "YEAH, I'M A FULL-BLOODED INDIAN." [I'D ANSWER]. BUT I HAD NO IDEA WHAT THAT MEANT.

EDWARD WILLIE, PAIUTE-POMO

Indian nations and Indian people today continue to benefit from the sacrifices made by the men and women warriors of Alcatraz. The federal government not only recognizes that a special governmental relationship exists between the United States and the individual Indian nations, but also that Native American people will no longer simply stand by and allow mistreatment and neglect.

Many problems continue to exist, however, and Indian people know that the battlegrounds of the future are in the areas of protection of natural resources; protection for Native American families and children; protection of treaty rights; and promotion and protection of tribal autonomy, sovereignty, and self-determination on Indian reservations, free from federal government intrusion and supervision. Many of the people who were involved in the Alcatraz occupation have gone on to become tribal leaders, attorneys, college professors, and journalists. Now, they apply their skills and experiences in attempts to reverse the tragedies and suffering of the past. Native American people have learned well the lessons of Alcatraz and Wounded Knee I and II. They are prepared for the future.

On the Alcatraz dock, May 1970, San Francisco resident Eldie La Banda Bratt, Quechua/Aymara from Peru, flashes a peace sign. (I. Hartmann)

IT WAS NEVER ABOUT MONEY... IT REALLY WAS ABOUT AN IDEAL.

JOHN TRUDELL, SIOUX

Recommended Reading

Deloria, Vine. *Custer Died for Your Sins.* Norman: University of Oklahoma, 1988.

Fortunate Eagle, Adam. *Alcatraz! Alcatraz!* Berkeley, CA: Heyday Books, 1992.

Johnson, Troy. *The Indian Occupation of Alcatraz Island and the Rise of Indian Activism.* Urbana: University of Illinois Press, 1996.

———, ed. *You Are On Indian Land! Alcatraz Island, 1969-1972.* Los Angeles: American Indian Studies Center/University of California, 1994.

———, ed. *Alcatraz: Indian Land Forever: Activism Poetry and Political Statements from Alcatraz Island.* Los Angeles: American Indian Studies Center/University of California, 1994.

——— and Joane Nagel, eds. "Remembering Alcatraz—Twenty-Five Years Later," *American Indian Culture and Research Journal Special Edition.* 18:4, 1995.

———, Joane Nagel, and Duane Champagne. *American Indian Activism: Alcatraz to the Longest Walk.* Urbana: University of Illinois Press [forthcoming].

Nies, Judith. *Native American History: A Chronology of a Culture's Vast Achievements and Their Links to World Events.* New York: Ballantine, 1996.

Smith, Paul and Robert Warrior. *Like a Hurricane: The Indian Movement from Alcatraz to Wounded Knee.* New York: The New Press, 1996.

Contributors

 **DENNIS BANKS,** Anishinabe, continues to work as a field representative for the American Indian Movement (AIM), an organization he helped found in 1968. It was as an AIM member that he came to the Bay Area during the occupation and met with participants as an expression of solidarity for their cause.

 **LANADA BOYER,** Shoshone-Bannock, was born on the Fort Hall reservation in Idaho. A mother (her son Deynon was with her on the island) and a student at UC Berkeley, she played a strong leadership role throughout the occupation. She later pursued a PhD and today, is in Washington, D.C., on a Congressional Fellowship.

 **ED CASTILLO,** Cahuilla-Luiseño, from southern California, was a junior facuty member at UCLA during the occupation and was among those who took the island on November 20th. After fifteen weeks on the island, he returned to college and later earned a graduate degree. He is now a professor of Native American Studies at Sonoma State University.

 **BELVA COTTIER,** Lakota Sioux, was one of the organizers of the 1964 Sioux occupation of Alcatraz, and advised the students as they developed their plans for the 1969 occupation. She is now retired from a nursing career.

 **TIM FINDLEY** was a reporter on the staff of the *San Francisco Chronicle* during the occupation, responsible for covering the various social movements in the Bay Area. He now lives in Nevada and continues to work as a writer.

 **ADAM FORTUNATE EAGLE,** Red Lake Chippewa, born and raised in Minnesota, was successfully self-employed and one of the leaders of the United Bay Area Council of American Indian Affairs. Now retired from his business, he lives with his wife Bobbie in Nevada and is an artist as well as a published author.

 **SHIRLEY GUEVARA,** Mono, was born and raised near Kings Canyon National Park, California. A student at Fresno State during the occupation, she is now an instructor at Hintil Kuu Ca Child Development Center.

 **MILLIE KETCHESHAWNO,** Mvskoke Creek, born in Oklahoma, relocated to the Oakland area in the late 1950s and was associated with the United Council during the occupation. She went on to complete the UC Berkeley film program and to establish herself as a Native American filmmaker and screenwriter.

 **WILMA MANKILLER,** Cherokee, was born in eastern Oklahoma and relocated to the Bay Area with her family when she was a child. As an adult, she became Principal Chief of the Cherokee Nation, the first woman in modern history to lead a large tribe. Now retired, she continues to be a powerful voice for her people.

 **JOSEPH MORRIS,** Blackfoot, was born on the reservation in Browning, Montana. A member of the ILWU and a working San Francisco longshoreman during the occupation, he is now retired and has written a book and produced several pieces of art.

JOSEPH MYERS, Pomo, was born near Ukiah, California. An Oakland police officer and then a state highway patrolman, he had returned to college and was in school when the occupation started. He is now director of the National Indian Justice Center and chairperson of the California Indian Museum at the Presidio of San Francisco.

RICHARD OAKES, Mohawk, was a iron worker before becoming a student at San Francisco State College. After leaving Alcatraz, he continued to actively work on behalf of native people; he died of a gunshot wound on September 21, 1972, during a protest in northern California. He was 30 years old.

BRADLEY PATTERSON was executive assistant to Leonard Garment, special counsel to President Richard Nixon. In 1969, his job was to work with Garment on matters of public policy, such as civil rights and Native American affairs. He is now retired from a long career in government service.

DON PATTERSON, Tonkawa, was born and raised in his tribal community in north-central Oklahoma. He relocated to the Bay Area in the sixties and was chairman of the board of directors of the San Francisco Indian Center during the period of the occupation. Today, he lives in Oklahoma and is President of the Tonkawa Tribe.

STEVE TALBOT, who received a PhD in anthropology from the University of California, Berkeley, was a volunteer instructor in the UC Berkeley Native American studies program previous to and during the occupation period, and was involved in early planning and support activities. He is now a professor at San Joaquin Delta College in Stockton, California.

JOHN TRUDELL, Sioux, was born and raised near the Santee Sioux reservation in Nebraska, and was studying radio and television programming at UCLA before joining the occupation. After it ended, he became active in AIM, acting as its national chairman from 1973 to 1979. After the death of his family in a fire, he withdrew and began writing poetry. He is now a published poet and songwriter, with a new album, *Blue Indians,* currently in production with Jackson Browne.

EDWARD WILLIE, Paiute-Pomo, spent his early childhood years on or near the Paiute Reservation in Nevada, and then relocated with his family to the Bay Area. When he was eleven, he and his siblings accompanied their mother to Alcatraz, soon after the occupation began; he was on the island for nine months. Today, he works at Hintil Kuu Ca, an East Bay child development center.

About the Author

TROY R. JOHNSON received his PhD from the University of California at Los Angeles and is currently on the faculty of the American Indian Studies Program and History Department at California State University at Long Beach. His most recent work is *The Occupation of Alcatraz Island: Indian Self-Determination and the Rise of Indian Activism,* published by University of Illinois Press.